THE
SHOOTING

Meredith Carson

World Codex Staff

The World Codex, LLC © 2018

Contents

PREFACE

"Constantly regard the universe as one living being, having one substance and one soul; and observe how all things have reference to one perception, the perception of this one living being; and how all things act with one movement; and how all things are the cooperating causes of all things which exist; observe too the continuous spinning of the thread and the contexture of the web."

Marcus Aurelius

The essential quotation above from The Meditations of Marcus Aurelius encapsulates the crux of the story you are about to discover, in precisely 66 words. As you explore the following account of James Wagoner - that number will take precedence - becoming key in this case study of SMR. You will begin to realize that the boundaries of Subjective Mystical Reality reach far beyond its innocuous sounding premise, into unexplored realms.

3

Although this recounting appears as an ordinary hunting trip shared by three close friends, both prey and predator are exceptionally extraordinary, and SMR plays a pivotal role in the telling. As you will see, the writing process produced some unsettling and unanticipated twists which even those intimately involved in the undertaking were unable to foresee.

Before I talk more about Subjective Mystical Reality, I'd like to introduce myself. My name is Meredith Carson, and the events that inspired me to write this book began this way.

After spending time in London with John Rollins, the dedicated researcher who penned the introduction to World Codex' novella, Lord of the Ring, and who offered evidence of the presence of a curse on the ring that inspired J.R.R. Tolkien's Lord of the Rings Trilogy, I returned to the United States for further research into material for my own work. In an odd case of paramnesia, after investigating the "continuous spinning of the thread and the contexture of the web," as stated above, I was inspired to meet a man who had a gripping tale to tell, but first I had plans to visit Mt. Washington in New Hampshire. I was desirous of delving a bit deeper into the origin and authenticity of a photograph that was shot there in 1870. That photo is purported to be the first image of a possible extra-terrestrial vehicle ever to be captured on film.

Ironically, while I was spending a few days at Mt. Washington, as I was exiting a hiking trail into the empty parking lot at the base of the mountain, just as you see in the picture on the back cover, I noticed an expensive digital camera lying on the ground. It appeared to me almost as though it had been intentionally discarded right on the pathway. However, as you can see in the photograph, there was no one else around anywhere. The camera was a Canon Vixia HF G10, and it was still switched on. The battery was almost dead, and the lens cap was missing.

I brought the abandoned camera to the local police, but I had downloaded the contents of the memory card into my laptop before doing so, out of sheer curiosity. When I viewed the photos - there were several shots of the area but nothing outstanding -

that is, until I came across the image you see on the back cover of this book.

Although I found the camera less than ten minutes after the time stamp indicated the picture was taken, I didn't see or hear anything odd when I reached the parking lot. An odor similar to the smell that is present after it rains permeated the air which I later discovered was most likely ozone. The scent lingered for several minutes even after I had found the camera. I surmised that perhaps the purplish blue hue emanating from the object's surface may have generated the sweet smelling fragrance.

The metallic looking object which appears to be hovering just above the ground, in juxtaposition to the mountain, immediately brought to mind the famous Tully Nests that had been discovered in Tully Australia in 1966. The town of Tully was just at the base of Mt. Tyson where the preponderance of UFO sightings by numerous witnesses had occurred that same year, and many years subsequent. A myriad of first-hand eyewitness accounts describing strange lights and extra-terrestrial vehicles were reported in that town over an extended period of time.

In that small isolated town in Queensland, Australia in1966, the first known modern crop circles were both documented and investigated as well. They are now famously known as the Tully Nests. The strange sightings there began with the Aboriginal people seeing what they called "devil men." They believed that if they were caught by the devil man, they would die. All of those incredible coincidences added up to more than just chance encounters, and I began to understand some of the intricacies I was faced with in my responsibility to cohesively convey them here.

Partly because I was invited to do so, and also because it is related to research and would most likely augment the breadth and scope of the novel which I have been working on for almost two years, I decided to author, The Shooting. Both books deal with cosmological, psychological, and experiential complexities regarding the nature of SMR. My extensive research is currently cataloged under the coded working title of Outer Manifestations of Inner Sanctity, or OMIS.

Much of what transpired during the writing process of The Shooting will be included in the novel as well, once I have digested its importance fully.

As I mentioned previously, I was inspired to meet a man who had a gripping tale to tell. The following story is based primarily on the shocking first-hand account of the events as recalled by him. His perspective is presented in the free-flow first-person narrative format which is without the interruption of chapters. The names used within have been changed, and any similarity to persons living or dead is purely coincidental. The writing staff at World Codex maintains a neutral perspective regarding the contents of this book.

Sincerely, Meredith Carson

THE SHOOTING

Initially, I intended to do all of the writing entirely on my own, but I eventually succumbed to the complexities of that task and sought outside help. Miss Carson, someone with whom I share many commonalities, did the majority of the writing and editing. This story is my personal account. It is an accurate portrayal of the events as they unfolded, presented with little embellishment.

The hunting trip portion of this book is where Miss Carson guided my method of conveying all that happened as vividly as I recalled it. Her interest and understanding of the subject matter came as a welcomed surprise to me, and the project has taken shape better than I had envisioned. James Wagoner is the name I have chosen to represent myself for the purpose of telling this impactful story, and I am a long time student of human nature. I don't claim to be a prophet, zealot, or political analyst. I am a proponent of SMR primarily, and that is where the soul of this book takes root.

My story begins beneath a calm sedentary surface - the exterior - the visible. Despite that perception, the more you pull back the curtain and peer inside - from the context to the subtext - the faster reality begins to morph into something that cannot be fully explained, or more accurately, defined. That is how I felt about all that transpired with my two friends and I as we embarked on what is now the focal point of The Shooting.

Events from my childhood have sculpted my aspirations and forged my identity, and that's where the heart of this uncircumnavigable treacherous labyrinth dwells. The completed puzzle of SMR is pieced together one intricate detail at a time. As the pieces begin fitting together, they will reveal much more than you may ever have imagined possible.

First and foremost, it would behoove me to point out that in my previous life, I was an avid hunter. What I mean to say is that before my life-altering incident, hunting was my only avocation and indulgence. I frequently bagged what I was after which was mostly black bear and deer, and I always returned from my escapades unscathed. Practical and tactical was my modus operandi, and patience paid off in the past more often than not.

Much to my dismay, and through the revelatory nature of events, my last surrealistic hunting trip ended in complete disaster despite my skill, stealth, and prowess. It wasn't the adverse conditions, topography, or the unexpected independent variables that caused us to fail so miserably. From my perspective, it was solely the superiority of the predator.

It pains me immensely to say that I am presently confined to a wheelchair for life because of all that transpired that fate-full fall weekend. To add insult to injury, and complicating matters even more - I have also lost 90% of the use of my right arm - as though experiencing some kind of mind-blowing nightmarish pseudo-reality. My injuries are the direct result of forces far beyond those which I imagine most everyone would be able to recognize or identify. I would never have believed such universal convergence possible had I not witnessed it for myself.

I should not be so surprised considering that my last misadventure was more of an expedition into the unknown than a hunting trip as it were. I do genuinely believe that at some point during the previous seemingly paradoxical fiasco, my two compatriots and I became unsure whether we were the hunters, or the hunted. In fact, through the process of reliving these events, I've come to the conclusion that we were a bit of both.

Initially, what the three of us were really attempting to accomplish was something that had never been done before, and in retrospect, I now admit that we should have set our expectations lower instead of inflating the probability of success based on our haphazardly executed plan of attack. Before I delve any deeper into all that happened, let me just convey that the pertinent events from my childhood which have molded me into the adult that I am today were paramount to the outcome of the trip. These insights from my youth may help to paint an enlightening picture of why we decided to embark on our misadventure together in the first place. Portents perceived from that picture may lend contextual understanding, much like how an old black and white photo from the past can convey a story through the scene that it has captured. An observer may catch a glimpse of what is to come from the subtleties and nuances of the old picture if it is scrutinized closely enough. I believe that such a keen perception is key to self-preservation and success, and it is a skill well worth cultivating.

From a psychoanalytical perspective, some believe that history ultimately predicts the future, but to me, that assessment of the nature of things appears to be little more than an oversimplification of events that are beyond explanation. It seems to me much like a rationale designed to explain away the complexities and extremes of human behavior which appears to often escape the most pedestrian perceptions of life. I tend to adhere to the understanding of all that matters most as something that can be cleverly assessed from a snapshot. The popular consensus being that a picture does indeed paint a thousand words.

An unrehearsed photograph can capture the truth because it reveals evidence of more than just what meets the eye. This is ironic to me since the word snapshot was initially coined as a hunting term, and I can relate to

13

that concept well. In the end, every individual must decide for themselves what is real and what is projected solely for the purpose of self-edification. It has been proven to me that It is often difficult to perceive the façade people emanate when posing in pictures where the image is used to convey confidence. Deeper hidden subconscious motivations are carefully concealed as our own hidden character flaws are rendered imperceivable through such deception.

What you see next is a snapshot of me just after I turned twelve. From my experience, perception about yourself and those around you comes to you in waves, like radiating energy in the form of light which illuminates the soul. The first radiating wave I can remember engulfing me occurred just two days after my 12th birthday when my father took me hunting for the very first time. My father had met that challenge, that same rite of passage with his father when he was the same age. I had learned that my great-grandfather Mortimer Latnem had set that milestone as a tradition many years ago. I suppose back in the 1800's it was partly an exercise in self-reliance, and partly a harbinger of the man you would become based upon your skill and success. However, it wasn't the hunting trip itself that conjured the magic, it was your very first kill that initiated the transformation from boy to man.

After I surrendered to the pressure of that inevitable forced transition from childhood into manhood, I learned some important things about myself. I've since come to understand that tradition may indeed be an inherent impediment to progress - if it is accurate that the only universal constant is change. I guess it was that kind of perspective that intrinsically caused me to resist participating at first. Despite my reticent ideas and hesitancy, the most important and surprising observation I made about myself through that initial experience was that I was born with a natural affinity for hunting.

On my very first outing, I had miraculously managed to shoot an eight-point buck, but the lackluster shot failed to kill the animal. That fact didn't seem to vex me as much as the idea that I had missed the opportunity to make my first one shot, one kill, which would have been a much more impressive debut as a hunter. Through what I now attribute to be an ideomotor reflex, I exsanguinated the deer with the brand new hunting knife that I had just gotten for my birthday. As I slit its throat, I can still remember how surreal it felt watching the life fading from its eyes - like trying to embrace the last glimmer of light from a diminishing sunset until it disappears into darkness, forever.

I learned quite a lot my first time out, but the story my father shared with me when he took me to an old abandoned gold mine was my second favorite thing that happened that day. My great-grandfather had worked in that mine sometime just before the turn of the last century. My father told me that there was still gold in it, but it would take too much time and effort to find and extract enough to glean a profit. He insisted that it was dangerous to go poking around inside the dark mine so he wouldn't let me take a peek that day because we didn't bring a flashlight with us. Undaunted, I came back alone many times after that to do some exploring and never told him about it.

Not far from that spot which was isolated and obscured from view almost entirely, there were some old rusty railroad tracks. The tracks disappeared into the overgrowth as though they led backward into the past, but they had at one time been burdened with valuable supplies for the towns that had sprung up when gold was discovered in the Klamath Mountains during the mid-1800s. One day, as my great-grandfather Mortimer Latnem was returning from the mine alongside those same old tracks, he saw something incredible, and I've never forgotten his story.

According to what my father told me, my great-grandfather enthusiastically described what he witnessed as a massive upside down mining pan made of silver floating just above the railroad tracks. My great-grandfather Mortimer Latnem had died before I was born, so I never personally got the chance to hear him tell his tale first-hand, but my father had asked him about it on several occasions and knew the story by heart. What my great-grandfather had witnessed was beyond any doubt a puzzling incident, and when I turned twelve, my father passed the account of fascinating events down to me.

In the early evening, Mortimer was riding his horse along the railroad tracks. He was heading home after working in the mine all day when he was privy to a spectacle that changed his life forever. He caught a glimpse of a huge silver disc as it floated just a few feet off the ground above the tracks, less than a quarter of a mile from where he was. The motionless object was poised directly in the path of an oncoming train which steamed right past him. When the engineer rounded the bend, he locked up the brakes as he was bearing down on it far too quickly. He frantically began blowing the whistle, but my great-grandfather reported that the disc didn't react at all, it just sat there hovering - silently suspended in the air right above the tracks - it just held its position almost as if it were defying the inevitable collision to occur. Anticipating some kind of imminent disaster, my great-grandfather cautiously started heading toward the potentially deadly conflux out of pure curiosity. He saw the heavy laden train come screeching to a halt just a split-second before almost crashing headlong into the mysterious object.

Unfortunately, according to what my father told me, hardly anyone really believed the story that Mortimer told, but he never shied away from sharing it nonetheless. He insisted that after the train had come to a complete stop, and as he watched from not too far away, he saw a fluctuating blueish glow and a bright flash of green light. The mesmerizing object then flickered for a few quick seconds and vanished into thin air. The locomotive was just sitting there on the tracks, motionless, and as Mortimer got close enough, he investigated why the train had not started to move again.

When Mortimer Latnem reached the train, the first thing that he noticed was that the engine itself had stalled which was beyond his comprehension. He shared with my father that what he experienced next gave him the "willies." These were his words, "I felt the hair on my arms rising, and then the hair on my head began to stand up. There was nobody on the train, no one at all, anywhere."

Mortimer spent several minutes calling out in hopes of a response but got none. He then gave up and headed back toward his home, stupefied, frightened, and bewildered.

After a while of sharing his story with friends and family, he consequently became saddled with the moniker, "Mad Morty." He also spent several days and nights in jail because he was initially suspected of having something to do with the missing engineer, but there was no evidence of foul play, and no body was ever recovered from the scene.

There were no other eye-witnesses to the bizarre event able to dispel or corroborate his story. Apparently, Mortimer Latnem was only guilty of being in the wrong place at the wrong time, and he suffered the consequences of that innocuous crime for the rest of his life through public ridicule and alienation. That unfortunate aspect of his tale almost brings me back around to my own more recent personal experience, except for one last important thing which was the most dramatic part of my first hunting trip and I'll never forget it for as long as I live.

At one point in our trek during the hunt, just before I killed that eight-point buck, and I say this without hyperbolizing, the most fascinating event of my life up to that point occurred. While my father and I were standing still and quietly scanning the forest for any movement, we spotted a Sasquatch not more than twenty-five yards away from where we were. Even now, I can still recall the chilling look he was giving us. No doubt he had spotted us first and had been watching us for several minutes. We were stunned by his enormity and the manner in which he projected his seemingly disdainful gaze in our direction. One can only assume it was aimed at our unwanted presence in his territory, almost as though from his perspective, we were trespassing.

Back at school, before I had learned to keep my mouth shut, I inadvertently followed in my great-grandfather's footsteps. I had regaled a teacher and some other students about our Bigfoot sighting. I was innocently and excitedly extolling the virtues of what my father and I had been privileged to witness first hand. I too had unwittingly made the mistake of assuming that those people were my friends and would accept my account and share in my enthusiasm. Instead, I, unfortunately, got made fun of and bullied as a result of my naivety. Over the years I have come to think of it as a kind of family curse.

The worse thing that I recall about our Bigfoot sighting was that my father had been wise enough to keep tight-lipped about it. That unforeseeable scenario made me look and feel even more stupid for saying anything to anyone at all. I guess everyone discovers at some point that, "hindsight is always 20/20." Afterward, I began to view my father, and society as a whole, in a completely different light.

The more time passes, the more clear some phenomena become in my mind's eye. I decided that sharing what it is that I have learned may be intrinsically insightful to others, and as a matter of fact, that's why I did everything I could to get this story into print. I must admit that I was still genuinely conflicted about how the subject matter may be received by those who were not there to witness events first hand. As my verve for life on this planet wanes, I chose to listen to my inner voice and express my thoughts come what may.

I imagine that many of you are a lot like me, in the sense that as soon as you hear of an unfamiliar acronym like SMR, you begin to try and guess what its implications are. So along those lines and to broaden the awareness of SMR and its potential, I chose to tell this story using its influence as the subtext, and I will expound on the gravity of Subjective Mystical Reality later. It suffices to say that because of my realization of its validity and its impact on my awareness of existential mechanisms, I now know that its power is immeasurable. Its ability to explain the complex impetus for the extremes of human behavior is astounding.

I'm not one who typically believes in a cautionary tale as a successful deterrent to foolishness, yet I concur inclusively with the idea that a smart person learns from their mistakes, while a wise person learns from the mistakes of others. Apparently, in retrospect, I have concluded that I am generally not a wise person, and it was only my exposure to SMR which brought me to that epiphany.

As my life surpasses its dreams and I'm left to fill my time with empty routines, I know more than ever that the details of what happened to me and my two friends need to be shared. Not so much for the drama or adventure of it all, but for its horror and enlightenment. I have assimilated from that experience this simple truth, real fear is sometimes the result of suffering from a lack of wisdom and humility. It is almost as though Newton's 3rd law of motion applies equally to free will and consequence, as it does to the physical attributes of matter. For every action, there is an equal and opposite reaction. In my case, the result of my vanity and pride has left me presently confined to a wheelchair for life. The sad fact of the matter is that for someone like me, it is as much of a mental burden as it is a physical one.

When I was contacted by R.W. Gates out of the blue, offering a professional author to pen this story on my behalf, I jumped at the chance as it were. Despite my infirmities now, the two other guys who were with me that weekend fared far less fortunate than I. As my account is the only record of what happened to the three of us, it is dedicated to the memory of them both. Their names were William Nordstrom and Michael Miller. It is my sincerest hope that Billy is still alive and well, somewhere, and that I may miraculously meet him again someday.

You may already be wondering, as some individuals at the Forest Ranger outpost initially were, if I was somehow responsible for the death of Mike and disappearance of Billy since I was the only survivor. Some onlookers even postulated that perhaps I was just too ashamed to admit all that had transpired. More than a few of those who were involved in my rescue, and subsequent inquiry, persist to this day in accusing me of having some kind of break with reality while out there in the midst of that madness. For the record, I tried to save Billy, Mike and myself from the throes of what we had stumbled across in the wilderness. Sadly, to this day there are even those who believe that I may have killed them both intentionally and that Billy's body will never be found. That is conjecture based on a lack of any evidence.

It is a well-documented fact, however, that in particularly hard to understand circumstances people refuse to accept what happens to others based solely on their version of events. That is why in cases involving jurisprudence the evidence is a vital component used in determining the truth. Otherwise, it is only an experiential awareness that gives credence to an incredible event when there is a lack of evidence to support it. In simpler terms, it is much the same as the old adage, seeing is believing. For those who weren't there, they will think what they wish based solely upon who they are inside and their level of understanding.

Although I managed to survive what happened, I'm forced to come to terms with the harsh reality that the three of us were faced with. I have suffered in many ways, not only because am I burdened with the long-term effects of my nearly fatal injuries, but also with the first-hand knowledge of what transpired. That situation vexes me more than I would have imagined; it has riddled my mind with guilt and unanswered questions. Be that as it may, those in authority still had difficulty in reconciling my maladies with my alleged malefactions. Their suspicions gave me pause to tell my story, but I needed to set the record straight for my own peace of mind. Retrospectively, I will always adhere to the idea that our fate was sealed before we even set out together that tragic weekend.

Mike and Billy were always more into adventure than hunting, as far as I was concerned. Proof of that was evident because on that trip I brought the only gun, my Remington 700. I also wore on my belt my hunting knife, and of course, I brought plenty of ammunition. The blade was the same one given to me by my father when I was twelve, and that particular rifle model was made infamous in 1966 by a man named Charles Whitman. He shot and killed 16 people and wounded 32 others from the University of Texas clock tower. For some reason, I found his story very intriguing. The fact that his address at the time was 906 Jewell St. and his murderous rampage lasted precisely 96 minutes, always fascinated me. Since the day I saw that Bigfoot when I was a kid, I've had a mild obsession with the odd occurrences of numbers, as I consider it to be a cosmological convergence of sorts. It's like trying to calculate the odds of being in the right place at precisely the right time.

The other two adventurers on our trek into the unknown were armed solely with some new technologies, fortunately, one of which was a gadget that ended up saving my life. I feel kind of sorry now for teasing my two friends about the things that they brought with them.

Mike was armed with a brand new Nokia cell phone, and Billy came prepared with a small device that he had heard about when he was overseas, called a PAL. He had even gone as far as to purchase stock in the company that manufactured it. While he was serving within the military intelligence community abroad, he got his hands on one of the early versions of the device and brought it with him on the trip, just in case.

PAL is another one of those unfamiliar acronyms that made me want to know immediately what it stood for. Billy told me that it stood for Panic Activated Locator and that technology is how they eventually found me. As far as I'm concerned everyone, especially children, should have a PAL. If the authorities hadn't used the signal from the PAL to locate me, I would have met my untimely demise in the grips of a protracted, excruciating nightmare, culminating in my death.

Since my amazing rescue, I've tried to get the word out encouraging the use of this technology for emergencies and to help prevent people from getting lost or abducted. So far, it seems that human nature is far too reactionary. The authorities would rather wait till someone goes missing and then endlessly search for them. As fallible human beings, we only seem to get worried when any given situation breaches the illusion of escaping the boundaries of our limited control, and sadly I regret to admit that I am no exception. Because I had my GPS and compass, I figured that with my navigational skills there wouldn't be any problems traversing the Klamath Mountains safely and successfully. Once again, my overconfidence about that assumption would ultimately serve to humble me even further.

Within a brief period, it became embarrassingly evident that I was also wrong about Billy's and Mike's other contribution to our three-man expedition. The first night when we set up camp, both Billy and Mike were wearing compact but very bright flashlights. Billy's was on his ball cap, and Mike had his on his shirt pocket. They were perfect for camping, yet I had never seen anything like them before. When I asked Billy what they were called, he gave me a quick smile, "Keep up with the times, they're wearable tech, and you need one now."

The hands-free lights were rechargeable using a small solar charger, and they employed lightweight magnets to stay affixed wherever you placed or wore them. Off the Grid (OTG) was what they were called, but they started out as "Streetlights" to be worn for pedestrian safety. I soon learned that when camping they quickly became essential for nighttime survival, especially when the unexpected wreaks its havoc in the darkness. Mike had also bought stock in the company that manufactured them, as Billy had done. I was the only holdout of the three of us, but today I have shares in the company's stock, as many as I could get my hands on.

We were set to embark on our excursion, and the Klamath River was turbulent, fast-moving and full. The melting snow from the warmer weather of late was sure to make our canoe trip more than a little treacherous. I had hoped that it would make the whole experience more fun, and Billy and Mike had been looking forward to it. Neither of them had ever displayed any lack of intestinal fortitude in the past or I wouldn't have asked them to accompany me in the first place. I was just more in tune with the environment overall, having had more experience under my belt.

I safely stored my compass and GPS in my backpack, as well as my own handheld flashlight. The other two were wearing their fancy new hands-free flashlights, and Billy's PAL was always around his neck on a chain that he used to keep his dog tags on. We were all set, geared up and ready to go.

As we climbed into my trusty old aluminum canoe, I took off my backpack to get more comfortable and improve my range of motion for paddling. The three of us couldn't resist clowning around about scenes from the movie *Deliverance* as we were beginning to head out into deeper water. We were winding our way downriver while Mike was poorly imitating the banjo music from the film, and the three of us were laughing hysterically. Then all at once, our fun turned into fear when the canoe slid up over a smooth rock just below the surface, tipping us over unexpectedly. All three of us were violently dumped into the river, along with all of our gear.

Frantically, we managed to rescue the canoe and both paddles first. Then I went after my backpack containing all of my clothes, my compass, GPS, and flashlight. It had filled up with water and went under before I could get to it. Billy and Mike had managed to capture their caps, but Mike's brand new cell phone fell out of his pocket and was lost. Overall, it wasn't really as bad as it could have been except for the fact that now we couldn't call anyone for help in case the need should arise. Any and all navigation was to be done mostly by the sun and stars from then on as well.

Knowing what I know now, that should have been the first indication that our hunting excursion may have been a bad idea from the get-go. We probably would have turned around and gone home had we not been lucky enough to retrieve most of the food we had brought with us. We also saved our water bottles, tent, sleeping bags, and most importantly, my rifle. So we decided to press on and try to achieve the seemingly impossible.

At this point, you may be wondering what it was that we were hunting in the Klamath Mountains of Northern California. By now if you think that it may have been a

Bigfoot, you are right. The Patterson-Gimlin film was shot on a smaller tributary of the Klamath River very close to where we were when the canoe flipped over. Bluff Creek is where we were headed, and I was determined to finally shoot and kill a Bigfoot, to conclusively prove to the world once and for all that they really do exist. I didn't want to end up feeling like my great-grandfather forever. His unkind nickname "Mad Morty" had always offended me somehow.

I have no way of conveying the strangeness - the converging factors which permeated the following events - but they were like a resonant wave that struck me. It started with the fact that my particular rifle model was linked directly to infamy in 1966 as I mentioned earlier, and coincidentally that I was born in August of that same year. The book entitled, *Do Abominable Snowmen of America Really Exist?,* was also published in 1966. Those three independent variables, on a metaphysical level, seem to offer some credulity to the synchronous thread that is explained by the ROPE theory which I have read more about since first learning of its existence. The book about abominable snowmen was written by the same man who filmed the now famous images of a Bigfoot, and some critics believe that the short film may have been shot during the same year as well.

The most fascinating and yet unexplained phenomenon that occurred the year I was born, and in the same month of August 1966, was the Lead Masks Case in Rio de Janeiro, Brazil. Two men, who were part of a group of "scientific spiritualists," were experimenting with some kind of extra-terrestrial communication and were later found dead as a result. Unfortunately, the only protection they were equipped with was a pair of homemade lead masks and ordinary raincoats. Their two corpses were found on a place called Vintem Hill just a few days after their experiment had gone awry. Several eye-witness accounts reported strange glowing lights in the sky above the hill that same night. The case has never been solved although I have my own theory as to what actually happened. Their secret project followed in the footsteps of others also exploring the boundaries of SMR several years earlier. Some of those pioneers had also died under similar circumstances and without any explanation.

I mention that case now because back when I was twelve, on that day when my father had taken me hunting for the first time, and we saw that Sasquatch, there was more to that story than I had previously shared. Just before we spotted the colossal creature, I caught the fleeting reflection of something otherworldly in a small pond right near where we were standing. It wasn't readily visible in the sky because of the tree canopy, but from what I could see in the reflection from the surface of the still water, like a liquid mirror, it reminded me of the object that my great-grandfather had described to my father all those years ago.

I hope this peek into the portal of my thoughts clarifies why Billy, Mike and I made this trip in a context that is easy to relate to. Not to be cliché or morbid, but it was almost a standard case of how curiosity killed the cat. Unbeknownst to them, I had always wondered if there was a connection between the two seemingly unrelated sightings. Because my father was intently focused on the Bigfoot, he never saw the thing in the sky, and I never mentioned it to him. Just as I caught a glimpse of whatever it was, he took a "pot shot" at the massive creature with his rifle. He referred to it as a snapshot, however, but I never acclimated to that kind of euphemism. My father often projected a sense of integrity with the use of that word when he missed what he was aiming at.

There is just one more thing that I failed to mention. My father's gun was the same one that I have now, my Remington 700. He left it to me when he passed away. He suffered from a brain tumor the year that I graduated from high school. Throughout his last twelve agonizing months, I watched as he slowly withered away and succumbed to his inevitable death.

As I stated earlier, the word snapshot usually conjures up images of photography. Although in the early 1800s, the term was initially coined to describe a shot taken with a gun, presupposing the necessity for aiming. It is a shot taken from the hip in a hurry which from my experience is never a good thing. That bullet my father fired wounded the Bigfoot we saw - but just like the deer I shot later that same day - the majestic creature didn't die right away. The behemoth took off running into the trees and out of sight, but we decided not to give chase immediately. A couple of minutes passed when we heard a loud roar off in the distance. It was apparent to me that we had provoked him into an angry rage. We gathered our focus and decided to track the intimidating animal to see how badly it had been hit by the one wild shot my father had managed to fire before it escaped into the forest.

Sure enough, about a hundred or so yards from where we had spotted him, we found drops of blood scattered on the surface of a boulder and some broken branches with bloody leaves strewn on the ground here and there. They were lying next to several monstrous footprints left behind in the soft soil around the base of the enormous rock. The footprints were awe-inspiring and unforgettable proof that we had not imagined what we had just witnessed. I'm not sure how big they were, but with my shoes on I was able to measure out three of my footsteps end to end, inside just one of them.

Mike, Billy and I were already friends at the time when my father and I saw that Sasquatch, and I told them what had happened. They were the only two friends that didn't ridicule me about it back in those days. As time passed, they became just as determined to find and authenticate the existence of a Bigfoot as was I. They believed my story without question, but that's because less than a week later, I brought them both out to the spot where it had happened. They saw with their own eyes the dried blood droplets still on the boulder, and the broken branches. The footprints wowed them just as much as they did me. Once again, as the old saying goes, "seeing is believing."

The physical evidence seemed to solidify the story for them, and that's why we all ventured out on our last fateful quest together. Although many others have seen these creatures too, still, there are many more who insist that they are only myth and primitive folklore. Some suggest that they may even just be another superstitious case of make believe, like alien abductions. Maybe it's better that people do think that way, because I am living proof that the Bigfoot population should be left alone, unmolested by human interference. They have proven to me that they are intelligent, intuitive, and highly perceptive. I have come to respect them as a species after what happened to the three of us during that last trip.

With only the two hands-free flashlights left after the canoe incident earlier in the day, we set up camp the first night about thirty-five or forty feet from the bank of the river. We were still wet in places from the slightly embarrassing mishap, and all three of us had parboiled looking feet from keeping them in our wet boots too long. To dry out our boots and heat some franks and beans from a can, we made a campfire which was well appreciated by that time. I estimated that we were within ten miles of where that Patterson-Gimlin film was shot, give or take. There was no moon that night, and I, of course, was the only one without a flashlight. Our senses were heightened, but we were tired from our impromptu swim in the river earlier in the day. All we were concerned with by that time was getting some decent sleep.

All three sleeping bags were opened and were still drying by the fire, so we left the embers burning when we bedded down for the night. It was difficult to get comfortable in the tent without our sleeping bags, but at least we were relatively warm and dry. We anticipated a rough night's sleep. Finally, we managed to drift off, but at about 2:30, Mike and Billy were awakened by a loud noise. From nowhere there came a sound like grunting, then a loud scraping, followed by a splash. I was outside the tent urinating in the bushes at the time, but it was so dark I couldn't see anything or anyone; I just stood there perfectly still trying not to make my presence visible.

The fire had gone out completely by then, and it was pitch black. I stumbled back to the tent in a hurry and grabbed Mike's light before he got the chance to get to it, and then I shined it around the campsite like a search beacon. I didn't see anything at all at first, and finally, Billy and Mike both got up and exited the tent. The three of us walked over to where the fire had been, and we were scanning the area using both of the lights. We held our tongues for fear of the unknown I guess, just trying to assess what had happened. Down towards the river and even up into the trees we were searching for anything out of the ordinary. Then Mike uttered these few words which sent a cold chill up my spine. In a low voice, he whispered, "Where's the canoe?"

Instantaneously, all three of us had the same paralyzing thought, but we didn't mention it to one another at the time. We all could sense that there was someone out there in the dark watching us. The nagging quandary vexing the three of us was what had happened to the canoe. It was fairly evident that it belonged to the river now, with or without any occupants. None of us were able to get back to sleep that first night. We just lay there until daybreak contemplating the inevitable consequences of losing our only mode of transportation. We never saw any signs of anyone being in the campsite, it was almost like a ghost had done the deed that would serve to put us into harm's way very shortly.

It became painfully apparent that if we were going to get back to where we had started from, we were now walking all the way. We estimated that we had probably covered almost fifteen miles on the river so far, but by foot, we knew that it would be much more difficult traversing the terrain. There were predominately no paths to follow, not that any of us were aware of. It was at that moment when I remembered that my compass was now at the bottom of the river somewhere; so we talked it over and decided to try and stay as close to its edge and use it for navigation.

That morning, after eating a cold breakfast and refilling our water bottles, we gathered up all of our gear and set off on foot. Our forward progress was slow going, to say the least. To make matters even worse, we were faced with high rock walls rising above the river bank and rocky terrain which was tricky and tiresome to traverse because we were carrying everything now. Although we took turns using the orphaned paddles as walking staffs, it was painfully evident that our progress would be tedious at best. We had plenty of food, and despite our unexpected dilemma, we hoped that maybe there was a chance we would still accomplish our goal.

We had been walking for about a half an hour or so when we started to catch a whiff of smoke in the air. Then, within fifteen or twenty minutes, we began to see a haze of black smoke in the sky. It had been very dry there the past few weeks, and it seemed that there was a brush fire ahead of us which was affecting a relatively large area. The upside was that we were hoping there would be firefighters present, with ATVs perhaps. After walking that short amount of time while carrying all of our gear, we decided that if it were possible to somehow hitch a ride back to where our truck was parked, we would capitulate and do it.

When we arrived at where the blaze was the most intense, we found it to be impassible along the river's edge. It became blatantly obvious to us that if we continued on our present course, we would be walking into the treacherous fire zone. The river had us trapped on one side, and it started to feel as though our options were the lesser of two evils. We would either be navigating through the thick forest - or trying to swim across the fast-moving river with all of our gear. Against the objections of my inner voice, we headed deeper into the woods to avoid the thick smoke and flames that were now beginning to engulf the brush and tall grass where we were.

We started to pick up the pace as best we could, but while attempting to traverse a tricky spot comprised of stones and small boulders, Billy lost his footing. He shifted his weight as he looked up through the smoke to catch a glimpse of what he thought was a bald eagle circling in the sky overhead. Falling hard, he let out a cry of pain and disgust at himself. After close examination, we all agreed that he had severely sprained his ankle. He took a few aspirins with several gulps of water and tried to calm himself. The three of us rested for a little while not saying much at all to each other.

It's amazing how important a simple thing like ice becomes in a situation like that when there is none available. The only consolation was that at least Bill was able to use one of the paddles as a crutch. We never did see any forest rangers or firefighters, but they would have been much appreciated at that point. The outcome of our trip would have been entirely different if we had been so fortunate.

While we were resting, we began pitching back and forth ideas about what could have happened to the canoe. From a distance, we heard a helicopter flying around somewhere but were unable to spot it. At that point, if I had caught sight of it, I would have tried to wave it down, at least for Billy's sake. I wish to God that I had been able to because a minute or two later our situation went from bad to worse. It felt like waking up from a nightmare only to realize that you're not dreaming - like a rushing gale force gust of wind that there is no way to steady yourself against had swept down upon the three of us.

We started out again, even slower now than before. Billy's ankle was severely swollen, and as it turned out - the big bird he had seen circling in the sky overhead wasn't an eagle - it was a vulture. There were several others in the sky and a few on the ground right where we were heading. In a charred section of grass, we saw something lying motionless which we assumed was a dead animal, but it was yet unidentifiable. The three of us cautiously made our way over closer to it, and after further inspection, we realized that it was the remains of a human body.

The vultures had picked away some of its flesh and plucked out both of its eyes. The scene was grotesque by any standard, and not more than twenty feet away there was another body which had been so severely burned that the three of us wondered if it may have been the initial cause of the fire. It was charred so horribly that we couldn't tell whether it was a man or woman.

The image of that scorched body made me recall a story I once read in college. It was a story by Charles Dickens called *BLEAK HOUSE*. In it, he described a case of spontaneous human combustion for which he later cited many historical examples documenting the rare but factual phenomenon. The body that we were looking at had the same morbid appearance that Dickens described in his story. With spontaneous human combustion, SHC, the body burns so hotly that the skull is left without flesh on it. Today that strange and rare occurrence is attributed to a preponderance of acetone which builds up in the body, and that looked precisely to be what we saw that horrifying day. The shocking and macabre mental picture is seared into my memory as an imprint of the visage that it once was, and remains clear in my mind's eye even now.

With some speculation, Billy, Mike and I reached the conclusion that these were possibly the two people who had attempted to steal our canoe. Perhaps they may have even just thrown it into the river during the night for the thrill of it. A sense of relief overtook us momentarily - until Billy facetiously quipped:

"Maybe they were murdered by the guy who did it, and then set on fire."

Instantaneously, we settled back into a fear-based reality which is hard to escape from - once it takes hold of you. I took comfort in the fact that I still had my rifle and that I was a pretty consistent shot with it. Even still, I was a bit worried, and for good reason. Much to our disbelief and terror - Mike met face to face the mysterious secret nemesis we were hoping didn't really exist. The elusive guilty party who had launched our unmanned canoe into the Klamath River made another appearance at our campsite later that night.

After we had spent enough time milling around those two dead bodies, we left them right where they lay and soldiered on. We decided it was unwise to disturb any evidence of a crime scene if indeed that's what it actually was. Because of the adverse conditions, and Billy's debilitating sprain, we were making progress at a snails' pace. Due to the smoke and fire, the route we were traveling took us continually further from the river, and not in the direction we needed to be heading. None of us could stop visualizing those mutilated corpses we had happened across. Try as we might, we were unable to collectively arrive at any sensible explanation for how those two people had ended up in such a horrible state out in the middle of nowhere.

When we had reached a safe place, far enough away from the fire, we stopped to rest for the night. A little while later, just before dusk, I climbed a tree to see if I was able to locate the river and gauge the distance we had traveled. Unfortunately, there was still too much smoke in the air to determine our position because the wind had died down quite a bit, causing a smoky haze to settle in the valley that we were now in. As far as I could tell, it looked as though the fire had more or less burned itself out in our proximity. I hoped that assessment would bring peace of mind and offer a few hours of well-deserved sack time for the night ahead, but that was not to be the case.

It was oddly quiet, too quiet. There wasn't even the sound of any animals. Most of the birds had evacuated the area, but it wasn't peaceful - it was just unsettling. The unnatural quietness felt more like the calm before the storm, and we had mistakingly attributed it solely to the fire and smoke.

The three of us had chalked up our failed excursion to bad timing and circumstances beyond our control. All we wanted to do now was make it safely home and share our adventure, or misadventure as it were, with family and friends. That was not to be the case either. The events that unfolded within the next few hours were as twisted as the course of the Klamath River - often out of control - and even more treacherous to navigate.

Without any moonlight, amidst the smoke-laden air, and under cover of night, every sound I heard, no matter how small, became unnerving. Camping in the mountains while being pursued by someone or something unknown feels a bit like wearing a blindfold and attempting to cross a busy street alone. To be honest, the whole nightmarish experience was becoming more and more terrorizing.

On that note, just a few weeks before the trip, I read a story that intrigued me. That tale was also unsettling in the same kind of way, and it felt a bit like something Dickens might write if he were alive today. It also reminded me of the situation Mike, Billy and I were in at that point in our surrealistic escapade. We were one step away from being in the throes of the fight or flight instinct, and by now our mission to find and kill a Bigfoot was beginning to feel inexplicably similar to that story. It was entitled, *Bigfoot Hunting.* It is apparent to me now from having been in almost the exact situation depicted in the frightening book - the title was indeed meant as a play on words.

It was categorized as a fictional story, but as a couple of my favorite sayings go, sometimes truth is stranger than fiction, and art does imitate life. The reverse of the latter is also true, so drawing the line between pure fact and fiction becomes exceedingly more and more difficult, and more than a modicum of truth is mixed in with almost every fictional story. I expected the book to be about hunting a Bigfoot, as the three of us had set out to do together, but reality is often much trickier than that. The nail-biting story detailed the account of two friends being stalked by a Bigfoot - and that's where it seemed the three of us had arrived. Something was stalking us, and we all knew it, although we didn't have the intestinal fortitude, or the wherewithal to admit it to ourselves just yet. The three of us were trapped inside that story, but we just hadn't come to grips with it wholeheartedly.

I suppose that is why the rangers and police who questioned me later about my account found certain aspects of it to be so incredible. It undoubtedly didn't help my case any that I was the only one found still alive, but what they didn't believe about my story mostly was the attempt that was made on my life, and how it happened. Sometimes I still don't really understand it myself. Then I catch my reflection in a glass door or something, and like my great-grandfather, the reality that I'm saddled with hits me square in the face.

As you may have already surmised, I have always loved to absorb the excitement of adventure stories, vicariously venturing into the unknown when I can. I love Charles Dickens for his subject matter and style, and he was clever with his diction and plot devices as well. The manner in which he depicted reality in his masterpiece, *A CHRISTMAS CAROL*, was brilliant. He managed to convey the context and influence of several supernatural manifestations as perceived solely through the eyes of the main character, Ebenezer Scrooge. Wholly altered by ghostly apparitions, his perception was entirely changed forever. That brilliant and insightful literary depiction of what one person can experience while others may never - is a prime example of SMR - and that is key to understanding the events that occurred next for the three of us.

We were all pretty tired that night after our arduous hike and the discovery of those two badly burned bodies, but I don't think any of us slept too soundly. It began to worry me more than I'd like to admit when again there was no moon, and as I mentioned, it was still much too quiet. Billy was in constant pain because of his ankle, and at some point, during the night Mike got up and left the tent to relieve himself. This time, since what had happened the night before, he was wearing his hands-free light on his cap. A minute or two went by, and I thought I heard a grunting sound. Then I heard rustling in the bushes close to the tent. A few seconds later there was a loud groan, and I saw Mike's light go out.

It got pitch dark and eerily silent except for the sound of heavy footsteps moving into the woods away from the tent. I grabbed Billy's light and trepidatiously stepped out of the tent, and as I did, I saw something or someone moving through the brush carrying what I assumed was most likely Mike. I was in a state of horror and disbelief. I called out to Billy, but he had no light, and his ankle was so badly sprained that he could barely stand without using a paddle to get to his feet. "Mike," I screamed out into the blackness but got no answer.

After arguing back and forth with Billy about what to do, we finally decided that it was too dangerous for me to head out into the woods by myself. With only one light left between the two of us, I decided to stay put for the night. If I chased after Mike, that would leave Billy alone in the pitch black tent for who knows how long. Even if I could hunt down whatever it was that snatched Mike away so quickly, I wouldn't want to fire at it and shoot him accidentally in the dark. We did our best not to panic, and Billy prayed that God would intervene on our behalf, somehow. We waited for dawn to break, and it felt like the night dragged on as though we were both on death row waiting for a stay of execution in the morning, for crimes we never even committed.

Sometimes even now, I wonder if that's why I survived and am presently tortured by being perpetually trapped in this chair. The whole crazy idea of hunting a Bigfoot for proof of its existence was mine. Both Billy and Mike were innocent by comparison. They lost their lives as a result of my selfishness, and the nightmare we were in was without a doubt my fault. The horror of Mike's abduction was exacerbated by the fact that the three of us had just passed the point of no return. It had finally become a matter of fight or flight, and I knew that this debacle was reduced to being stalked and hunted. Our attempt at killing a Bigfoot had morphed into nothing more than a matter of survival; it was a case of kill or be killed.

The rest of that night Billy and I talked about what our next move should be. Finally, we agreed that he would stay there at the campsite during the day, and I would venture out with my rifle and look for Mike. Billy was convinced that if he made a fire and kept it burning, he'd be safe there by himself. I, however, was not so confident.

The dawn finally broke, and after making a mental picture of where the campsite was, I set out with just my rifle, some water, and a few granola bars. I left Bill with his light and my hunting knife, and then I headed out alone to look for Mike. Before I took off, I told him that I would return before dark come what may, unless I was detained against my will, or dead. I reminded him to answer me loudly if he heard my voice later, in case I had trouble locating him. We used to employ that same call and response technique to find each other when we would play in the woods together as kids.

I had just left Billy when much to my surprise, about ten feet from the tent and caught in some bushes, hanging off the ground, I found Mike's cap and light. The light had been switched off. So, I clicked the button, and it flickered on much to my relief. At least I knew I had a light that worked if I was still out searching by nightfall. After about fifteen minutes of wandering, I did see some broken branches here and there. I surmised that I had stumbled across a trail that was left behind by whomever or whatever it was that had absconded with Mike during the night. I didn't find any evidence of blood however which was a huge relief.

Tracking as best as I could, I realized that I was beginning to encroach on some familiar looking massive boulders that were hidden behind a grove of tall trees. All at once I got a feeling of déjà vu. It was at that moment something told me that I was close to finding Mike. My heart began beating faster, and fear started to creep in as I imagined what scene I might uncover, thinking about those two bodies I had seen the day before. I couldn't seem to get that gory picture out of my mind. Then from somewhere very close, I heard a crunching sound from among the branches strewn on the ground, and I froze in my tracks.

Moaning sounds were emanating from in-between two giant boulders, and it was just at that moment I realized I was at the old abandoned gold mine I had visited many times as a kid. As quietly as I could, I stealthily stepped toward the huge rocks and passed through the entrance of the mine; I switched on Mike's light which was still affixed to his cap which I was now wearing. Weirdly, as I stepped over the intimidating threshold from light into darkness, it felt like I was passing through a portal backward in time.

Since I had my gun locked and loaded, I decided to take a chance and call out Mike's name to see if I could get any response. "Mike," there was just silence, "Mike," I called out once more. I heard a voice not too far off which was barely able to utter an audible response. At that moment, at least I knew that it must be Mike and he was still alive. I cautiously walked deeper inside the mine, and there he was lying on his back with his eyes wide open. Even at first glance, I could tell that he was in a lot of pain. He entreated me in a pathetic voice, "James don't touch me!"

In a voice not much stronger than a whisper, Mike described to me how he was grabbed from behind and then rendered unconscious by being struck in the back of the head. Unfortunately, he had no idea who had done it. He told me that when he regained consciousness, he was right where I had found him, paralyzed and in pain. He assured me that it didn't hurt too badly if he didn't try to move at all. We both assessed that his back had most likely been broken. Now my anger was beginning to intensify into a rage, but I simultaneously felt a wave of helplessness and realized that he and I were caught in the middle of events that were far beyond our control.

I had no idea how to handle the double bind I found myself faced with. I couldn't move Mike, and I couldn't stay there and leave Billy behind by himself armed with only a knife. I would never wish a choice like that on anyone. Whoever or whatever it was that was terrorizing us was going to get shot come hell or high water. That was the only resolution I could muster. Everything else in my head beyond that was just guesswork or conjecture. By then, there was more than a reasonable amount of panic seeping into my thoughts and clouding my judgment.

Out of the blue, I came up with a plan. I asked Mike if he thought he could aim and fire the gun. He said yes he thought he could do it ok. So I gave him the rifle and instructed him to shoot the sneaky perpetrator, twice, if they should come back into the mine. Mike managed a weak smile and agreed. I told him I was heading back to get Billy, and that we would both return soon. The plan was to construct a makeshift stretcher and to try and get him safely out of there. I handed him the gun and left him with some friendly, yet serious advice, "Shoot straight," I said. My conscience bothered me thinking that I was leaving him alone, lying there helpless like live bait, but we both agreed we had little choice in the matter.

Before I walked away, it dawned on me that I still had Mike's light, so I turned around to pass it to him before I made my exit. He smiled with relief and shared with me that the darkness was alive with evil possibilities in that damp abandoned old mine. Mike aimed the light at the wall to point out something I hadn't noticed.

"Look at that." I turned around and examined the inside of the shaft for the first time since I had been a boy. Both he and I were shocked at the scene we were privy to. It immediately became challenging to reconcile the distinction between animal and human, but it became clear that something or someone had been living in the mine for an extended period of time.

There were bones strewn about on the dirt floor, yet some of them appeared to have been sharpened, as though they had been made into tools or weapons. The most puzzling thing was that there was an

Ouroboros etched into the wall which is an image of a snake eating itself. The snake was encircling a maze surrounded by strange, unfamiliar symbols and a series of numbers. None of it was recognizable to me even though I'd been in that mine several times all those years ago.

It was almost as though Mike and I were privileged to a quick glimpse into some foreign world; it was like a flash of crystalline evolution depicted in distinctive detail before our eyes. I imagined it to be akin to an artist's unveiling of a never before seen priceless piece. Momentarily, I took back the light from Mike and used it to study more of the bizarre scene. We were stunned and in disbelief by the debris scattered on the floor, and the unintelligible markings on the wall. Having been there before, I was shocked by all of what I was seeing because it was new to me. I thought that maybe I had just never noticed it back when I was younger, but the gravity of it seemed to hit me all at once.

The darkness of the mine and the expanse of the caverns were assuming an ominous presence, but I put my fears aside and continued to try and take it all in. My curiosity got the better of me once again. Beneath a fractured rock, there was an opening leading into what looked to be underground caves. I would have loved to have investigated the enigmatic site even further, but I had to get back to Billy so we all could get away from this surreal place as fast as possible.

Survival for the three of us was paramount at that point, and I knew that it was up to me to get us out of there alive if I could. Again my conscience was beginning to bother me because I was responsible for the situation at hand, and I knew it. Just before I gave the light back to Mike, and set off to get back to Billy, I noticed one last thing that both confounded and amazed me.

There was a stone protrusion coming down from the ceiling about the size of a blackboard, ten or twelve feet off of the floor. It was apparent that it wasn't part of the old mine. There were no wooden supports, and it appeared to be a natural formation integrated with an arched dome-shape which transitioned into two stalactite pillars. To me, it almost seemed to resemble some kind of upside-down altar. I remembered seeing it when I was a kid but didn't think much about it then. This time, upon closer inspection with the bright light, I could see that there was writing inscribed into the rock. I was fascinated because it had completely escaped my attention before. I stood there silently for a few seconds, and then read what it said, loud enough so that Mike could hear me.

8 BECOME 1 – A KEY WAS FOUND –

AN EXPRESSION OF 3 – TO ETERNITY

Below that there was an encircled number 13. And just below that, what I saw next, I was utterly unprepared for. I couldn't even believe my own eyes. There, carved into the stone by hand, were two simple words, Mad Morty. Mad Morty, the unfortunate nickname my great-grandfather had received after witnessing the unbelievable incident with the locomotive and the mysterious shiny object, way back before the turn of the 20th century. That memory hit me like another wave. It caught me off guard because my father had pointed out to me a couple of times that the 20th century was the 10th and final century of the second millennium which was a two thousandth anniversary, as it were, of the crucifixion of Christ.

I didn't have time to try and figure out what I had just read, and what it all meant, but I did notice that there were thirteen words written in the first part of the inscription. I also noticed that Mad Morty was eight letters, so I guessed that 8 become 1, could possibly mean one, as in an individual. If we survived this ordeal, I intended to return to the abandoned mine and intently explore the caverns that it was adjacent to, but for the time being, it would have to wait.

I realized that I had wandered away from where Mike was, so I had to tear myself from my uncanny surroundings and get moving. I hurried back over to him and found him unconscious. I wasn't sure at first if he was still alive, but when I nudged his shoulder, he opened his eyes. He had missed everything I had said to him before. I handed his light back to him for the last time and said.

"Here, hang in there." Then I imparted to him one more thing before I took off for the campsite.

"Don't worry, I'll be back, I promise."

I walked out of the bizarre scene as though I was walking out of an episode of the Twilight Zone.

I hadn't yet eaten a thing and was beginning to feel hungry, thirsty and weak. After I had walked about a mile or so, I decided to rest for a few minutes and eat something. I picked a soft spot under a tree, opened up a granola bar, and quenched my thirst with the cool water. I leaned back and gazed upward at the big beautiful oak. As I was surveying its size, I caught a glimpse of something that was hung up on one of the branches about fifteen feet off the ground. It was black and had an undefined shape; I couldn't tell what it was. I stood up and scanned the grass around me for a stick long enough to push the mysterious object out of the tree.

I poked at it several times until I managed to free it from the branch, and as soon as it fell to the ground, I could see that it was a moldy old backpack. All sorts of crazy thoughts ran through my head as I imagined how and why it may have gotten tossed up into that tree. The first two questions I wanted to have answered were how long had it been up there, and what was inside of it. It felt like I was discovering a secret time capsule. The answers to my questions came reasonably quickly. It was easy to determine how long it had been perched up in that tree because inside of it, among some dirty clothes and an empty box of crackers, there was an old Polaroid camera from the 1980s. I found some faded pictures too. From that piece of outdated technology, I was able to estimate that the backpack had been up there for approximately a decade or so.

Two of the pictures were of a young woman, so I rifled through the backpack to see if there was any ID or information to indicate who it may have belonged to. The only other thing I found inside was a well-worn paperback book. It looked like it had been used quite a bit, perhaps in college. Needless to say, I was both intrigued and perplexed by the curious find.

Leafing through the pages of the book, I discovered that it had been a gift given to someone named Karen. The inside cover had a dedication which read as follows:

"Dear Karen, this book helped me reach my full potential - I hope it does the same for you, your friend, Jim."

At that point, I surmised that the backpack had belonged to the woman, Karen, although it was hard to tell from the dirty crumpled clothes left inside. Some of them looked like they had belonged to a man instead. It was another puzzling thing that I came across that weekend.

I had heard about a girl who had gone missing back in 1989. A woman named Karen Hansen was reported missing by her ex-boyfriend back when I was working as an associate professor. The administration and students had organized a search party and handed out flyers, but to this day her body has never been recovered. Her ex-boyfriend, I believe his name was Murphy, had informed the police that she had met someone new at school and he suspected him of being responsible for her disappearance. Murphy was the prime suspect at the time of her abduction, however, and as a result, he killed himself by jumping off a bridge six months later. Most everyone assumed that his suicide was an admission of his guilt. From examining the backpack, I couldn't tell whether it was Karen Hansen's for sure, or not. I really had no idea either way, and it seemed to me that it could have belonged to anyone.

To be honest, I must admit that the book I found in her backpack intrigued me more than her story. So I rested back down on the moss under the big oak to take a closer look at it, mindful of the fact that Billy was waiting for my return ASAP. It had only been about ten minutes or so since I had stopped to rest, so I figured I had a little bit more time to spare. I was careful not to get too comfortable because the moss was beginning to feel like a bed to me at that point, and the day was warm and sunny. The subject matter of the book intrigued me too much to ignore the impulse to read some of it. It was entitled, *SMR: An Exposé.*

I must admit that I wanted to read some of it to satisfy my self-indulgent nature. I had been familiarized with Subjective Mystical Reality in college, and I found that it was something else that I had an innate affinity for. I remembered that there was a chapter I had really enjoyed previously exploring. I found myself immediately drawn back to the explanation of the specific scientific nature of the Double Slit Experiment. It is a fascinating empirical exploration of subjective reality.

I was reading about how the act of observation by one entity, alters the reality of another's existence without any detectable level of interaction whatsoever. The experiment itself is changed just by anticipating the predictability of its outcome. Therefore, by merely believing that an event can be compromised or manipulated through simple observation, or a shifting perspective, then ipso facto, it is. For lack of a better explanation, the phenomenon is apparently caused to occur through unseen powers of the cosmos.

That unexplained phenomenon led to similarities pertaining to the nature of the Heisenberg Uncertainty Principle which was discussed at great length in the following chapter. The book expounded, describing how the two theories are likened to a kind of interactive metaphor which when fully grasped can affect many aspects of life. If such principles are effectively applied, they can and will produce a reality which is both subjective and mystical. By conjuring a realm where the metaphysical and existential become manifested into the physical, they result in a deep dark rabbit hole, not unlike the one Alice tumbled into through the imagination of Lewis Carroll.

As I was contemplating the complexities and pondering the possibilities of the powers of personal perception, I heard a startling grunt that came from directly behind me. In an instant, something struck me on the back of the head, and I was stunned. When I was able to get up and look around, I was flummoxed by the fact that there was no one there. My first thought was that I had no weapon because I had left my rifle with Mike and my hunting knife with Billy. My instinct told me to climb the big oak tree to get off the ground, and as an ancillary benefit, I could increase my field of view and perhaps spot who had hit me. I managed to get up about twenty feet, and then I saw movement in the brush about seventy-five yards or so away. It was blatantly apparent to me that it would be unwise to give chase at that point, still being dazed and completely unarmed.

Then, much to my dismay, I realized that it was becoming dusk. I grew aware that I must have drifted off to sleep while I was reading that book, or blacked out when I was struck. When I looked at my watch, I was shocked to see that three and a half hours had slipped away from me so quickly. I soon came to terms with the fact that I had no flashlight, and all I could think about was getting back to Billy before the darkness engulfed me.

There was finally just a sliver of moon visible, and at least the cloud cover was light. I estimated that I must have had three or four more miles to go to reach the campsite where

I had left Billy, all alone. It worried me that the entity who had struck me in the back of the head with a rock seemed to be moving in the same direction - toward the campsite. Out there somewhere, lurking just about the length of a football field ahead of me was my nemesis. I could sense that it was waiting for me somehow, but what choice did I have but to continue.

My head was beginning to throb now, so I shoved the book into my back pocket and took off toward the campsite. It was hard to blink because my eyes were burning. I expect that sensation was due to my fear as I was anticipating almost anything now. It was bizarre, but a panicky feeling, almost as though I had been there before and was facing death, began to fray my nerves. My nerves were a rope that was starting to become unraveled, and by now, this whole nightmare was beginning to feel like a pre-ordained exercise in terror which may have been orchestrated by some kind of madman, or demon. Maybe something even more significant and beyond my comprehension was stalking me, and it felt as if it were bearing down on me now. I would have tried to escape if I could have, but neither the footing nor the brush was conducive to any prolonged quick progress. Night was approaching, and it was getting darker by the minute.

I took some deep breaths and through my innate propensity to rely on experience, I managed to clear my thoughts enough to think tactically. I saw a tall tree not far from me and scaled it to increase my field of view before it got too dark. Scanning the horizon, I hoped to spot the tent somewhere not too far off in the distance. Fortunately, Billy must have charged his light during the day with the solar charger because the inside of the tent was illuminated. I could see that there was a campfire already burning, and I relaxed momentarily.

From near the treetop, I had a clear line of sight. I could tell that I was only a couple of miles away from the campsite. Across the rough terrain and combating the quickly approaching darkness, I figured it would take a little less than an hour at the most to make it there if I didn't lose my direction along the way.

I did my best to pinpoint the location of the tent using the stars. I could almost place it just below the center star in Orion's Belt which by then had become visible in the night sky. I calculated that if I walked toward that center star, I would end up very near the campsite. I would yell out to Billy as I got closer, and I would look for the light. At least, that was how I envisioned my plan unfolding.

By the time I made it back down out of the tree, it was almost totally dark. This time, I set off resolutely. Now that I had a navigable path ahead of me I was hopeful. Although it was more difficult traversing the terrain while attempting to maintain a straight line toward Orion's Belt, I felt reasonably confident. I was walking slower, but at least I knew where I was headed. I tried to keep a steady gaze up at the stars as I trudged along. I hadn't covered much ground when I heard the sound of two pieces of wood being struck together. I had read that a Sasquatch uses that method to ward off humans who venture too close to their habitat. It is a primitive communication device called "wood knocking." At that point, my senses were on high alert, but I did my best to maintain my composure and focus on the task at hand.

There are quite a few theories on what a Sasquatch or Bigfoot really is. Some assert that they are shapeshifters, while others insist that they are interdimensional beings. There are those who even claim that they are most likely some kind of alien-animal hybrid. Regardless of which possibility is correct, I have always considered them to be enigmatic, but with the propensity for violence under the right conditions. My opinion at that time was based on the manner in which the only one I ever saw looked at my father and me on that first hunting trip we took together. It instilled both fear and respect with just one quick glance. What happened that last night out in the wilderness only proved my theory to be correct.

While I was navigating by the stars, I saw something beyond belief in the night sky; it looked just like what I had seen when I was a kid. It seemed to be hovering above where I was heading. It was motionless for a minute or two, and then it flashed and vanished out of sight. A couple of seconds after that visual spectacle - I heard wood knocking again - and this time it was even louder so I assumed that I was getting closer to whatever it was that I should have been trying to avoid.

I stopped walking and gazed upward because something was happening above me unlike anything I had ever seen before. Another object, moving fast through the sky, had emerged from behind me. It passed almost directly over my head and then began to slow down. It was massive, and its altitude was very low, but it made no sound whatsoever. I have never been privileged to such an astonishing sight before, and I held my breath until I consciously made myself exhale again. My heart was pounding.

From the bottom of the object, a beam of yellowish-white light was projected downward onto the ground. It lasted only a few quick seconds and then disappeared altogether. While this was going on, I completely forgot about the wood knocking sounds I had heard just prior to the astounding extra-terrestrial event.

While I was fixated on the unexplainable scene in the night sky, my situation had drastically worsened. A few seconds after the beam had disappeared - the mesmerizing object in the air over my head did the same. As Mortimer Latnem vividly described, I could feel the hair on my arms and head rise up like it was reacting to a vastly powerful charge of static electricity. Then the vehicle shot upward faster than any rocket I'd ever seen - until it faded from view and into the expanse of space.

I never saw anything like that before, or since, but I will be able to picture it perfectly in my minds-eye, always. Just as it was back in my great-grandfather's day, I got the feeling that nobody would ever believe a word I said when I shared that information with them. If they had been there with me, however, I know that they would have been as amazed as I was. Later on, when I was being questioned by authorities about the events that took place, I got the impression that my credibility may have taken a hit with the addition of my UFO sightings. I could have kept them to myself, but that's not my nature, so I told them everything just as I witnessed it. I went on to describe to them what I experienced as the events unfolded.

For a brief moment, I wondered if Billy too had seen what I saw, or perhaps he saw the one that had passed over where he was. My guess was that he was in the tent and missed everything, but I was hoping he could verify it so that everyone wouldn't be inclined to believe that I had hallucinated it all due to the stress I was under. Getting to my destination was proving to be an uphill battle, and I was just at the foot of that hill at that moment.

As soon as I could focus my attention back on my destination, I set out again. I took a few short steps and then heard loud grunting. It was more like a growl to my ears, and It startled me. I was caught off guard and immediately aware that it was almost the same sound I had heard earlier when I found the backpack in the tree. It became clear that I was being either surveilled, stalked or both. The latter of which seemed logical to me because that's what I would be doing if I were on the hunt.

Considering how dark it was among the tall trees and thick brush, there was no way I could see anything at all. Something inside was compelling me to run now as fast as I could. It felt like the fight or flight instinct had finally taken over my body. So I ran for my life towards the campsite that was waiting for me under the center star of Orion's Belt. That's where Billy was, and the flashlight that he had. Most importantly, he had the hunting knife that I had left with him, and I wanted that weapon now in the worst way.

I was doing my best to keep up my quickened pace. My goal had changed from running toward a destination to one of running away for survival and escape. There were intermittent grunts and the sound of branches breaking behind me, so close that I was too horrified to stop under any circumstances. I came up over the top of a small hill and caught a glimpse of the tent, and the light was still on inside. I was getting close to reaching it safely now, so I pressed on with all of the strength and endurance I could summon. At one point in the chase, I could swear I heard heavy breathing right behind me, but I dared not turn around to see what it was. I just kept running.

I called out, "Billy, Billy," as loudly as I could, but he didn't answer. I saw his campfire still barely burning about five-hundred yards away, and I knew then that I could make it if I just didn't give up and slow down. As I got close enough to smell the fire, I sensed that whatever had been chasing me had dropped back and ceased his pursuit. I collapsed on the ground, winded and still frightened, but too fatigued to take one more step. I was within fifty yards of the campsite now, and proud of myself for not having given up, and given in.

I took out my water bottle and swallowed the entirety of what was left in a matter of seconds. A couple of minutes passed, then, breathing deeply, I got back to my feet and very slowly started off again to find Billy. As I got closer to the tent, I began to suspect that something might be a bit off-center with the seemingly serene scene. Everything was in place, and the light was still on inside the tent creating a soft glow on the canvas. I noticed right away that there was no shadow - no movement inside the tent at all.

Although I couldn't see Billy anywhere, my eyes panned the horizon as best as they could in the darkness, trying to take in everything that was still visible. Nothing was making sense to me. I tried once more to evoke a response by calling out his name, but there was only a deafening silence. If it were not for the soft hoot of an owl somewhere perched in a tree close by, I would have felt that a predator was still hiding somewhere close enough to finish off both Billy and me, once and for all.

When I finally reached my destination, I hesitatingly drew back the tent flap and looked inside, but just as I had expected, there was no one there. Billy's cap and light were on the floor, as were his shoes, socks, and all the rest of his clothes. They were all in a pile as though they had been dumped out of a bag and onto the tent floor, but he was gone. His PAL was also on the floor among his discarded clothing. I picked it up, and his cap and light as well. Then I scanned the tent for the hunting knife. I found it underneath his clothes at the bottom of the pile, so I grabbed it and exited the tent. I called out his name once more, but still, there was no response. I decided that since I had the light and the knife now, I could try to do a one-man grid search for him rather than sit around and wonder where he had gone. I had begun to consider myself armed and dangerous.

The light was reassuring and exceedingly helpful, much to my surprise, and I didn't see any sign of anyone or anything unusual at all for that matter. Casting my gaze to and fro as I walked, several minutes had passed when I was once again startled by a loud growl. I reacted and started to instinctively make a beeline back to the tent, to stoke up the fire and keep watch from there. I fled for my life - because as they say - discretion is the better part of valor.

I was startled by the proximity of the sounds around me, and subsequently, I must have momentarily lost my bearings. I turned around and picked up my pace taking a few significant quick steps. Without any forewarning, the ground below my feet fell out from underneath me, and I felt my body descending into a black void in the earth.

As I dropped, the cap and light flew off of my head and landed in the grass above me. My body impacted a large rock, and I suffered a loud, jarring crunch. In that instant, I was unable to move my right arm, and it was suddenly too excruciating to even try. So I clenched my teeth and resigned myself to the intense pain. I was fighting as hard as I could not to give in to the temptation of crying out for help. My thoughts drifted back to Mike for a second, not because I was worried about him, but because I realized that he and I were in the same situation now. Both of us were paralyzed and helpless.

Apperceptions began to manifest themselves as fears, as I wondered if we both would remain in our current state, pathetic and stranded, until death came to claim us. A mental picture entered my mind of both our skeletons and how they would be found someday, many years later, probably by some innocent hikers out enjoying the scenery. Or even worse, perhaps no one would ever find either one of us. At that moment, for all intents and purposes, it felt like both Mike Miller and I were on the brink of oblivion.

Then there came another wave - like the first one that had ever hit me - only this was more of an awakening. I imagined that it was almost as impactful as a near-death experience. It was more intense than when I slit that deer's throat and held its head in my hands until it died. This wave nearly drowned my senses. I was dumbstruck for the next five minutes of my life, and the images still strike fear and wonder into the depths of my soul even today.

Looking up from the bottom of the pit, I could see its edge illuminated by the light that I'd lost when I fell into the fifteen-foot deep hole in the ground. The surface illumination gave off an eerie, surreal glow to my immediate surroundings. I was, for a few seconds, and for some unknown reason, mesmerized by the winged insects that were flying around - passing freely in and out of the glow that was radiating above the pit.

Surrounding me, there were a dozen or more human skulls and skeletons strewn all about the bottom of the pit. I suddenly became aware that it was a trapping pit, and I was the prey this time. Not only was I paralyzed, but to be honest, I grew frozen by both pain and panic. Horrified at the scene, it felt like I was experiencing an out of body nightmare. I could almost look down at myself, and see my body skeletonizing before my eyes.

I wondered if Billy was trapped inside my mortifying nightmare as well, somewhere very close by. Maybe he was also lying in this pit, already dead, naked and in the early stages of decomposition. I did my best to try and get an accurate picture of the remains I was in the midst of, but couldn't see him anywhere. As I lay there motionless, surrounded by human bones and skulls, it felt as though they were beginning to watch me. I struggled to concentrate on arriving at a plan to try and make it out of that pit alive, and then, much to my horror, I realized that this wasn't just a trapping pit. It was some kind of mass grave which opened up even more macabre possibilities - too many for me to even begin to contemplate.

Piercing the darkness and silence, I was plagued by the sound of grunting. I knew that this time there was no way I could escape from it. I held my breath and stayed totally motionless, waiting. Without moving my head at all, I cast my gaze upward, and I saw a giant Bigfoot standing at the top of the pit, poised on the edge and peering down at me intently. The eerie light produced a shadow across his face, making him look like he was entertaining a smile which seemed to be generated by some hint of grim satisfaction. It gave me chills, but I couldn't turn my eyes away from him.

A second later, I became transfixed once more. From out of the darkness, there appeared another hulking figure. It stood next to the first, but it was holding a stone that must have weighed at least a hundred pounds. I didn't move a muscle. I couldn't move. I was anticipating the impact of the massive rock, and I knew it would be the end of me. My thoughts flashed back to when I was a kid, and my father had wounded one of the behemoths. I could only think that perhaps I had fallen victim to some kind of vendetta. At that moment I think I succumbed to shock because things are a bit blurry in my mind.

I knew that there was nothing I could do. I didn't call out or beg for my life; I just watched and waited. My thoughts flashed back to the writing and strange markings on the rough-hewn walls of the old mine as the seconds seemed to tick by like hours. From nowhere and without any warning, the Sasquatch dropped the heavy stone into the pit directly at me, missing my head by just a few inches. I did my utmost not to react at all. The two monsters must have been satisfied that I was dead. A minute after I felt the thud from the stone as it slammed down next to my skull, both of the creatures disappeared from my field of view, vanishing back into the darkness. I've seen them several times since that terrifying night, but only in my recurring nightmares.

A white light shone down brightly upon me. At first, I imagined that it was an angel, and I envisioned that I was dead, or dying. Then I came to my senses just enough to realize that it must be a rescue helicopter. I was elated at the possibility of a rescue. The light blinded me, yet it became frighteningly clear that there was no sound accompanying it. It was then that my mind began to fantasize that I was on the brink of being abducted by some alien entity, but instantaneously the light disappeared as quickly as it had come. I opened up my eyes to scan the sky, but I didn't see or hear anything.

Because of the stress and trauma that I had incurred, both physically and mentally, I'm not sure if I had really seen that beam of light, or I had somehow only imagined it. I've never expressed the level of fear that I suffered during those hours I spent in that pit, until now. I admit that it makes me wonder about the fate of my friend Billy Nordstrom. His body was never found, and I often imagine and hope that we will meet again someday because I believe he is still alive. The pile of his clothes that were left behind in the tent were the only evidence that he had been there at all that night.

As I lay there in the mass grave, contemplating my impending protracted death while silently reliving mind-numbing events, I thought about how bizarre it was that Billy had vanished without a trace. Then I remembered something that had previously escaped my thought processes entirely. I realized that I still had Billy's PAL in my pocket, his Panic Activated Locator. I reached into my pocket and pushed the button twice.

Feeling woozy, I finally blacked out from the pain as it was intensifying immensely by then. I have no way of knowing how long I was in that pit, but when I regained consciousness, I was informed by the head of the medical staff that I was safe in an infirmary subsidized by the state of California. I was still unable to move my legs, but I was fortunate and thankful just to be alive.

Since my rescue, I've been relocated to an assisted living facility that is also owned and operated by the state of California. The doctors and staff here have been gracious so far, but I haven't been informed that I can leave as of yet. Due to my compromised physical state and the necessary care required for me to function from day to day, I am content to stay right where I am for the present.

Most everyone here has been friendly toward me. However, there are a couple of men that continue to pester me with questions. They are from the FBI, or so they tell me, but I do have doubts. I placate them as best I can when they come around to talk to me. I've shared my story with them many times, but it seems that no matter how many times I regale them with my escapades into the unknown - they are still intrigued and want to learn more details. I've begun to get the distinct impression that there is a psychiatric wing here somewhere and that they may be involuntary guests. In all fairness, I humor them as best I can when they make their quasi-entertaining appearances.

I was surprised to learn that the charred corpses Billy, Mike, and I had discovered that weekend were hikers and that they had inadvertently started the fire which spread amazingly fast because of the high winds. At least that's what my two persistent visitors explained to me, although it seemed as though they were unsure about it still. They described how both men had gone missing right around the same time the three of us were on our disastrous hunting trip. I made it clear to them that the only connection between those men and ourselves was that we were all adversely affected by the wildfire and that we had not crossed paths previously.

They also informed me that the SMR book I had in my possession when I was rescued had belonged to a woman named Karen Hansen which was not news to me. Although much to my surprise, I hadn't remembered that the inscription on the inside cover was penned by someone named Jim. When they asked me about that, I told them that I always go by James, because I sensed what they were implying. They informed me that the girl was reported missing over a decade ago. I didn't mind telling them that I remembered her story, and if I wasn't mistaken her ex-boyfriend was the prime suspect although they never managed to find enough evidence to convict him of any crime.

They showed me her picture and then told me that her skull and skeleton were both found in the same pit that I was pulled out of that horrible night. Her head had been separated from her body postmortem as far as they could tell. They also shared with me how her dental records were used in determining her identity, and that it was indeed Karen Hansen. That kind of forensic technology is so important when it comes to solving a murder. I congratulated them on their discovery, and I wished them luck with their ongoing investigation into her disappearance.

The two men had jogged my memory. I remembered a girl in my modern philosophy class at college that I had helped with a paper she was writing, regarding the varying degrees of subjectivity concerning experiential edification. I recall that she seemed to think I had a unique perspective on the topic and was interested in learning more about it. I'm pretty sure her name was Kathy though, looking back on it now. My college teaching days were so hectic that it's sometimes hard for me to keep all the names and faces straight in my mind.

The two consistently inquisitive men who dressed in suits reminded me of *Men in Black*. They repeatedly asked me what had happened to Billy. I didn't have an answer because I didn't know, but for whatever reason, they refused to believe me. Finally, after having told them the same story several times, I quipped.

"I think Billy Nordstrom is somewhere beyond the exosphere."

They didn't seem to appreciate the humor, but I thought it got my point across well. I had posed this question to them.

"How was I supposed to know what had happened to Billy when I couldn't even find him myself? I fell into that trapping pit or a mass grave, or whatever it really was while I was searching for him in the darkness by myself, under duress."

I also asked them both this question, to which I could get no rational response.

"If I knew where he was why would I be out there in the woods at night, stumbling around in the dark looking for him?"

To this day, I can't understand why they are still unable to comprehend that fact. I have a feeling that his disappearance will never be solved because some mysteries are meant to be beyond the realm of human comprehension. I've come to accept that fact after all I have done and seen.

During one of our last conversations, and out of pure curiosity, I baited them into seeing if they may indeed truly be FBI agents because I had my doubts. They seemed to me to be more along the lines of NSA perhaps, or something of the like. So, I asked them a simple question that only one other person in the world should know the answer to.

"How many skeletons were there in that pit, altogether?"

They confided in me, with a fair amount of certainty, that there were thirteen skeletons found in total. I thought that was ironic. It struck me very odd that the number 13 was encircled and inscribed on the wall of the old mine not far from where I had left Mike. They never pointed out that fact to me, and I never mentioned it to them either.

Thanks to Billy and his electronic PAL, I am here to share my story with all of you. The others who were not as fortunate, are forced to remain silent forever, never getting the chance to offer their accounts, to tell how they ended up dismembered and decaying in that pit. My two informative acquaintances had shared with me that some of the bodies had their heads removed, and some others were missing arms, hands and feet. According to the two agents, it took more than three full months to piece together the myriad of skeletons and bones. They did their best to make sense of the macabre collection of murdered victims and to identify some of the bodies.

The one thing that bothered me the most, and it felt like they were harping on it when we talked, was what had happened to Mike. They told me that they eventually located his body inside of an abandoned mineshaft, but he was found headless as well. Mike was identified by his fingerprints, but as of yet, authorities have not recovered his head. I found it a bit repulsive how they shared that kind of information with me considering how horrific that image is.

The search for Mike's missing head is still ongoing. Over time, their questions have adversely affected my sensibilities more than I would expect. I've become repulsed and incensed as they continue to inquire if I had any idea where it might be. One of the annoyingly persistent men told me that there was writing on the cavern wall in the proximity of Mike's body which again I was already aware of. He seemed somewhat pleased to inform me that lab technicians were currently testing and analyzing all markings and materials that were found and collected at the scene. In an offhand way, I admitted that I recalled some writing, and I inquired to which he was referring, exactly. Out of the same morbid curiosity that caused me to study those two burned and mutilated bodies we had found, I needed to try and understand what may have happened to Mike after we parted company.

I was taken aback when one of the agents handed me a scanned copy of a wrinkled piece of paper that he said was a page ripped out of an old book. The book had been torn into pieces and found on the floor of the mine next to Mike's corpse. After I read the words written on it, I became apoplectic and declined to speak with either of them any further about what had happened to Mike. I was beginning to suffer nightmares from reliving specific events that the three of us endured on that disastrous hunting trip.

Later, although I was still offended by the innuendos they seemed to be aiming in my direction when we spoke, I requested that I may keep that copy of that disturbing page. Much to my surprise, both agents agreed, and every once in a while I feel compelled to take the haunting piece of paper out and read it aloud. I will share it with you before I conclude this account of my experiences. It vexes me immensely when I try to figure out which book it is from, and precisely what it means. Deep down I have a sneaking suspicion it once belonged to my great-grandfather, Mortimer Latnem. When I consider the context of that page, my thoughts are always the same. Only some kind of egomaniacal narcissist, or psychotic serial killer, could compose something so Machiavellian in nature.

INVISILIQUE

A subjective reality deception primarily executed through smoke and mirrors, not overt or obvious, and often over-looked - that which appears as assimilated through subtext only; hidden via facade produced by actions which serve as diversionary devices

Example: **Mercy of the Executioner**

"I, the executioner, grant unto you new life -- as I lop off
your empty head...
Freeing you from your worldly strife – making sure, once
and for all, you are dead!"

Latnem saw god Live- the reverse is reality
? 6 words + 6 become 1

AUTHOR'S NOTES

The two "FBI" agents who had visited with James Wagoner on several occasions had very strong suspicions regarding the accuracy of events which culminated in his incredible tale. The subsequent miraculous rescue from the mass grave where he was found only supported their theory about his involvement. Because of his apparently exaggerated accounting of events, and vague timeline, they were able to deduce with almost complete certainty that he was untruthful about much of what had transpired.

In light of those incriminating circumstances - both agents felt as though pressuring him further may, in fact, lead Mr. Wagoner to attempt an escape from the psychiatric ward of the state hospital - where he was being held for an indeterminate amount of time. They were granted permission to execute a clever trap for him, and it succeeded, but not without further unforeseen tragedy.

Less than one week before he fell victim to their covert plan, a small tracking device was placed in the lining of a down jacket that he curiously kept as a remembrance of his experiences. As anticipated, he attempted to make his get away with only a few personal items, mostly clothing, and some monies he had kept well hidden in his room.

Immediately after Mr. Wagoner was discovered missing, the two FBI agents who had been intentionally vexing him with their interrogations were contacted by the police department. The small tracking device was remotely activated, and he was apprehended shortly via a police helicopter search patrol. James Wagoner was located at a roadside diner apparently making his way back toward the Klamath Mountains. It was speculated that he was en route to perhaps destroy evidence of his crimes.

When he was captured, he was wearing the down jacket which sent out the locator signal that pinpointed his location. The scenario was ironically much like the one that saved him from the mass grave he had fallen into. When initially questioned by police, Mr.

Wagoner had only this to say to the officers who made the arrest.

"I realized my mistake when describing a scene to Miss Carson during the writing process. I knew I was in jeopardy as soon as the words left my lips. Without thinking, I said this to her. 'Remember, the weight of a gun matters most. When it's heavy, it's full of potential because it's loaded. When it's light - make sure you've wiped off all the fingerprints - and collected all of the shell casings.'"

James Wagoner had intended to make his getaway across the Mexican border after retrieving whatever it was he had left behind in the Klamath Mountains. His Manifest 13 was to be his self-edifying story, the accurate account of all that had shaped his life, and his actions. He overestimated his cleverness, however. When he murdered the night nurse and made his escape, he sealed his own fate. In a bizarre coincidence, he and Mrs. Schaffer shared a commonality - they both were born the same year, 1966.

Wagoner was indicted for Mrs. Schaffer's murder. His manifesto was used as evidence against him during his extensive trial. When asked, the FBI agents who planted the tracking device told reporters that they had noticed the bottom of Mr. Wagoner's shoes were a bit worn. That is when they came to the realization that he had been able to walk for some time. They presumed that he most likely also had the use of his right arm, more so than he led others to believe. Wagoner had used the wheelchair as a disarming device to gain sympathy, but they had suspected that it would be only a matter of time until he made his move. Mrs. Schaffer's death was the only crime Wagoner committed that was able to be proven through the evidentiary trial process. Subsequently, James Wagoner was sentenced to life in a maximum security prison without the possibility of parole.

The events leading up to his escape happened as follows. On the morning of his flight, the day after his last intense questioning session by the two FBI agents, it came to the attention of the shift supervisor that the night nurse on duty had not reported back to her station after her shift had ended.

Earlier that evening, James Wagoner had been served his dinner, consisting of steak, potatoes and green beans; everything seemed normal. At 6:45 a.m., an orderly, Mark Lundquist, attempted to open the door to Mr. Wagoner's room. That door was never kept locked as it was the safety protocol for wheelchair patients to leave the room readily accessible in case of an emergency. Mr. Lundquist discovered that the door was indeed locked, and when he knocked, there was no answer. The diligent orderly immediately became concerned, and within minutes he retrieved the key to open the door

Much to his relief, when he unlocked the door, he found a person in bed with the covers pulled up over their head, yet there was no movement at all. Mr. Lundquist announced his presence but still got no reaction whatsoever. He began to worry that perhaps Mr. Wagoner had died during the night, or even more likely may have committed suicide using his round tipped, serrated, semi-sharp steak knife blade. The orderly was wrong on both counts.

With a justifiable amount of trepidation, he carefully drew back the covers and was horrified at what he saw. There in the bed was the night nurse who had failed to report back to her station at the end of her shift. The contusions on her neck and bruising on her face indicated that she had been struck several times and then most likely strangled to death. The disheveled room contained several profound clues to what had happened, but Mr. Lundquists' reaction to what he found caused him to leave the room hurriedly. The police were immediately called, and not long after the two FBI agents who had been questioning James Wagoner the previous day arrived at the facility.

The room was cordoned off, and a team of crime scene technicians began to examine and collect all of the evidence. In the meticulous process of gathering up everything, they found Mr. Wagoner's chilling Manifesto 13. Mr. Wagoner penned his Manifesto 13 and left it as a taunt to investigators without realizing he had been targeted using a tracking device. His accurate account of all that happened was in the manifesto he left behind. It has become the basis for the very in-depth case study in Subjective Mystical Reality.

After close examination, it was determined that most likely the title,

Manifesto 13, is related to the fact that the opening line contains thirteen words defining SMR. It was also pointed out during Mr. Wagoner's trial that there were thirteen skeletons found in the mass grave from which he was rescued.

I am relieved that this ordeal is finally over. I spent many hours in a small confined space alone with James Wagoner, and I am fortunate to still be here to convey to you all that I have come to understand. I will refrain from expounding any further regarding my thoughts and theories; perhaps the pages of Mr. Wagoner's manifesto are far better suited for such insights. There are still many aspects of his account that are yet unexplained. As for me, my research continues.

Meredith Carson

MANIFESTO 13

SMR is a state of being with parameters far beyond boundaries of geocentricity. That simple truth was my awakening. For the record, I would like to point out that over time the connotations of SMR have expanded to include more concrete terms - as well as contemporary aspects of our modern technology - but its fundamental principles remain much the same, "unfettered and alive." Its application has been downplayed by governments and dogmatic organizations since its introduction to the geopolitical world stage almost a century ago. If truth be told, what I have done under its umbrella is of little consequence in the vast configuration of things.

Based on what many people are inclined to believe, the Zodiac Killer's reign of terror began to take hold in California in 1966. Several other unexplained events converged during that same year. In SMR, there exists a labyrinth, and at its center is the cosmological intersection of those outwardly unrelated events. Even now some of the most frightening and mysterious aspects interlaced within that synchronous thread are seemingly beyond my own comprehension. Many of them have the same common denominator, the year of their occurrence, 1966. That being the year of my birth, I took it as a sign of my destiny.

A month after the murder of Cheri Jo Bates, a typed letter entitled "The Confession" was sent to The Daily Enterprise newspaper, which is now The Press-Enterprise. The letter gave an eerie account of the murder and contained accurate details of the crime scene not yet released to the public. Many believed it was from the killer. Six months after Bates was killed, a handwritten note was mailed to Riverside police and The Daily Enterprise. It simply said, "Bates had to die. There will be more."

After reading about that chain of events, the idea came to me that I could commit a similar sensational crime and gain notoriety someday as well. Not long after I had exsanguinated that deer on my first hunting trip, I began to imagine that notion becoming a reality. That is also about the same time that I began to covet my father's Remington

700 hunting rifle. My thinking at that time was that I may someday have a book written about my escapades, and perhaps a movie as well. This is the material which I envisioned being noteworthy, and I didn't have any desire to settle for small-time articles in a newspaper like the Zodiac Killer.

The fact that I have an IQ near 150 is probably why I was able to determine who the individuals involved in the Zodiac Killer case were. It strikes me odd that even now the investigators have missed the thread that exists between the four individuals interconnected, and the obvious link to Charles Manson. Carved into a boulder on the Spahn Ranch is the symbol used by the Zodiac, and no one ever mentions that fact. I took a photograph of it in the early eighties when I visited there.

When Charles Whitman killed those people in Texas, in 1966, I took it as another sign. As I grew older, I watched my father getting weaker and sicker. Ever since he had left me twisting in the wind, as it were, when I needed him to back me up after seeing the Sasquatch, I decided to expedite his slow agonizing death. When I was alone with him in the house, I suffocated him to death and took his rifle as my reward for helping him to reach his destination sooner, without any further unnecessary suffering.

Unfortunately, for some reason unbeknownst to me, my mother began to suspect me in the expedited death of my father. I'm not sure to this day what it was she thought - but I was never very fond of her - and as a result, it didn't require much for me to end her well-justified suspicions. She was strict and unsympathetic with me as a child, not an empathetic woman by nature. I felt as though she never wanted me because I somehow came between my father and her.

Several months after my father's passing, when I was a senior in high school, she instructed me to get gas in her car so she would have enough for work the next day. I obeyed her wishes like the dutiful son she expected me to be. When I returned to the house, while she was making supper and such, I opened her brake lines. Her drive to work the next morning took just about a half hour, and most of the route was rural with winding roads. While on her way to work in the morning, she apparently lost control of the car and hit a maple tree head-on. The car was totaled, and my mother was comatose when they found her. She was rushed to the hospital but succumbed to her injuries several agonizing days later. She had never been a proponent of seat belts, even when I was a kid.

The passages from my story about the UFO sightings are real, just as I described them. I've come to understand that the dates and circumstances of such occurrences are the quintessential factors that cause such anomalies. I'd like to give an example of what I mean.

During the Great Fire of London, in 1666, there were many reports of bizarre sightings in the skies around the city and surrounding areas. By 9/6/1666, news of the fire had traveled as far as Berwick, which is located north of London. Local soldiers there claimed that they had seen visions of "ships in the air." Reporting the phenomenon back to Whitehall, one Mr. Scott assured his contact that he believed it to have been just their imaginations, but he did not seem to be convinced of that fact himself. It is also a well-documented fact that approximately 13,000 homes were destroyed during the Great Fire.

The encircled number 13 in the cave and other writings were etched into the walls by me. I am confident that my great-grandfather, "Mad Morty" had spent time in that abandoned mine as well because I have no accounting of some of the markings on the walls. The snake eating itself was not my creation.

The page from the Raven Paradox was torn out of a book I borrowed from the local library, back when I was at school. That is when I met Karen Hansen. She and I were friends, but I began to detect that she only had interest in me as nothing more than an acquaintance. Eventually, I grew weary of our disappointing assignations and did my utmost to frame her boyfriend for her untimely death. I convinced her to come with me to see the Bigfoot evidence that I knew existed out near Bluff Creek. That is when I took her life and left her backpack as evidence of the crime.

It came to my attention later in life that 66% of Americans were in favor of the death penalty, so I only assumed that it was an indication of its essential role in my dogma. I became the executioner for those who refused to adhere to fundamentals which are necessary for survival - survival of the fittest. That's when I began to lure people out to the wilderness and kill them. The pit where I dumped the bodies was well hidden. The night I was looking for Billy, I got startled by the predator who was stalking me and fell victim to my own deadfall trap. Believe what you will about the disappearance of William Nordstrom, I had nothing to do with it. I did not have many people I would consider friends, but he was one.

Two strangers had inadvertently met Mike, Billy and I when we set up camp the first night. One of which was Karen Hansen's older brother Mitchell. He recognized me, and I became suspicious about his presence and timing, not being sure of who his friend was either made me feel uneasy. That first night I threw our canoe into the river because I had snuck out earlier in the night to locate the two uninvited men. I found them both and threw all of their gear into the river after I had set them on fire using the accelerant they had handy for starting campfires.

Mike was abducted by what was, I can only assume, the same Sasquatch that heaved the massive boulder down into the pit at me. I know that part of my story nobody will believe, but it is true nonetheless. I have no reason to lie. I do not understand how Mike Miller was murdered, or what happened to his head, but that was not my doing either. Things are going on out in the Klamath Mountains that are mysteries still. I hope Meredith Carson will find the answers she is seeking. Perhaps I will live long enough to read her novel when it is released - I am in it.

Thank you from World Codex staff!
If you enjoyed this 2nd book
in the SMR series -
check out Book #3 now available on
Amazon!

OR

If you also enjoy audiobooks -
Sample our breakthrough audio:
Codex SE

Now available on
Amazon, Audible, & iTunes!

SMR Book 3: Burning the Scarecrow